In the Clouds

Written by Susan Reid
Illustrated by Virginia Barrett

Jake O'Brien wondered why he hadn't noticed before. The branches of the old oak tree were a perfect shape for a tree house. He could imagine it there already. He asked his father, "Dad, can I build a tree house in the oak tree?"

Mr. O'Brien thought it was a great idea. "But you can't spend much money on it," he said to Jake.

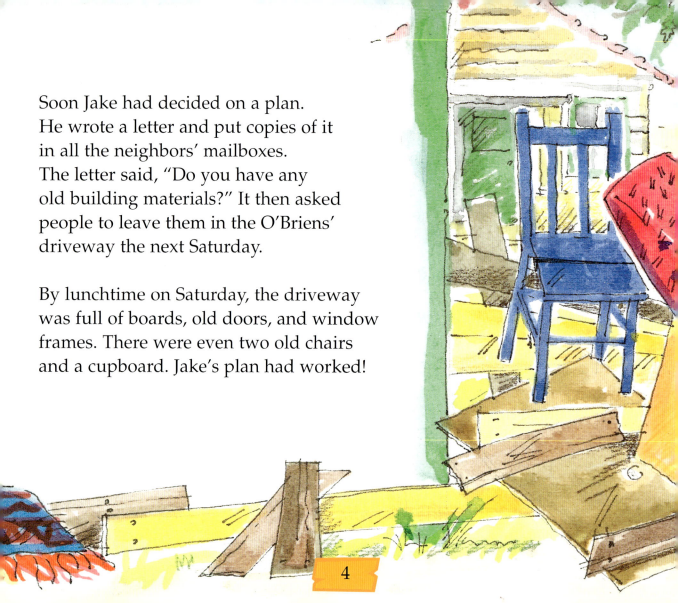

Soon Jake had decided on a plan. He wrote a letter and put copies of it in all the neighbors' mailboxes. The letter said, "Do you have any old building materials?" It then asked people to leave them in the O'Briens' driveway the next Saturday.

By lunchtime on Saturday, the driveway was full of boards, old doors, and window frames. There were even two old chairs and a cupboard. Jake's plan had worked!

"Jake, I'm not sure I like this idea of yours," said his mother.
"What are we going to do with all this junk?"

"Well, we'll have to look at it all, and then we'll have to take what we don't need to the dump," said Jake.

"You mean *I'll* have to take it to the dump," said his father.

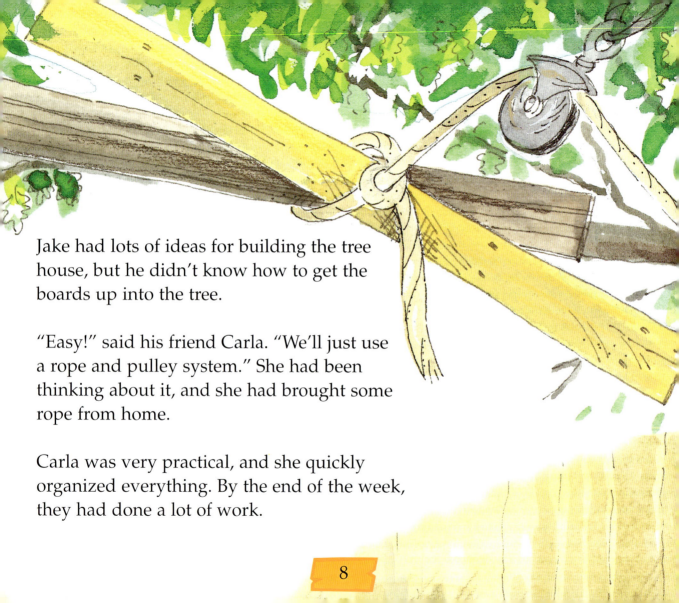

Jake had lots of ideas for building the tree house, but he didn't know how to get the boards up into the tree.

"Easy!" said his friend Carla. "We'll just use a rope and pulley system." She had been thinking about it, and she had brought some rope from home.

Carla was very practical, and she quickly organized everything. By the end of the week, they had done a lot of work.

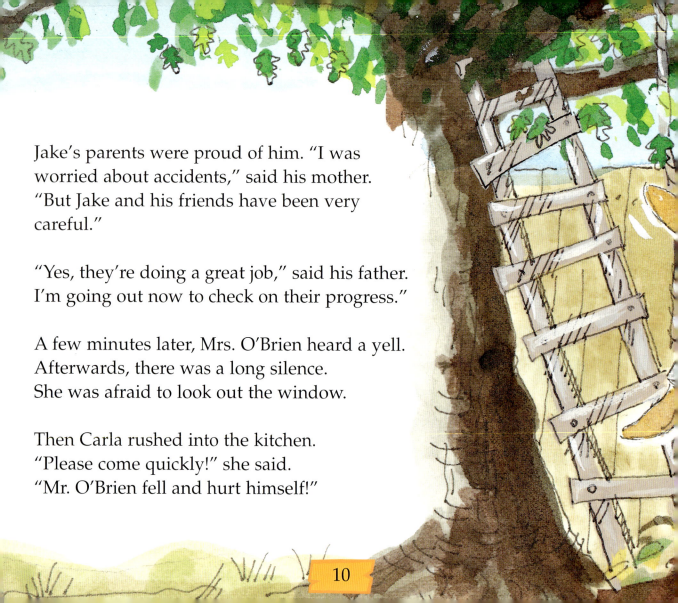

Jake's parents were proud of him. "I was worried about accidents," said his mother. "But Jake and his friends have been very careful."

"Yes, they're doing a great job," said his father. I'm going out now to check on their progress."

A few minutes later, Mrs. O'Brien heard a yell. Afterwards, there was a long silence. She was afraid to look out the window.

Then Carla rushed into the kitchen. "Please come quickly!" she said. "Mr. O'Brien fell and hurt himself!"

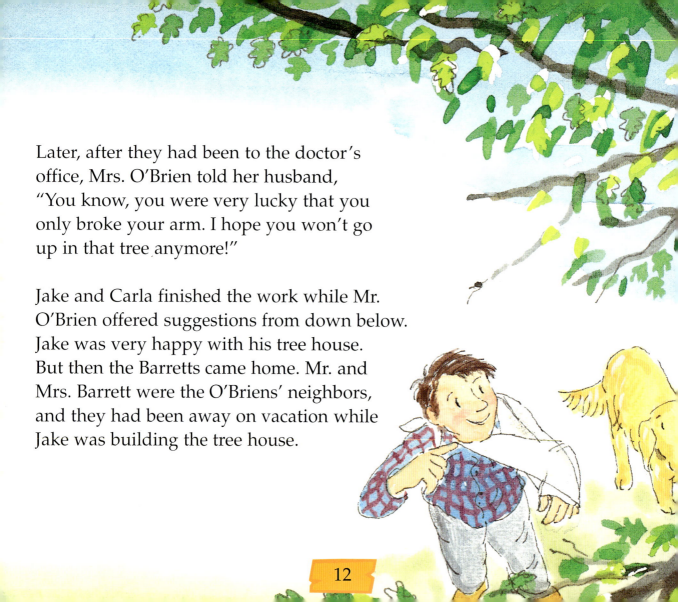

Later, after they had been to the doctor's office, Mrs. O'Brien told her husband, "You know, you were very lucky that you only broke your arm. I hope you won't go up in that tree anymore!"

Jake and Carla finished the work while Mr. O'Brien offered suggestions from down below. Jake was very happy with his tree house. But then the Barretts came home. Mr. and Mrs. Barrett were the O'Briens' neighbors, and they had been away on vacation while Jake was building the tree house.

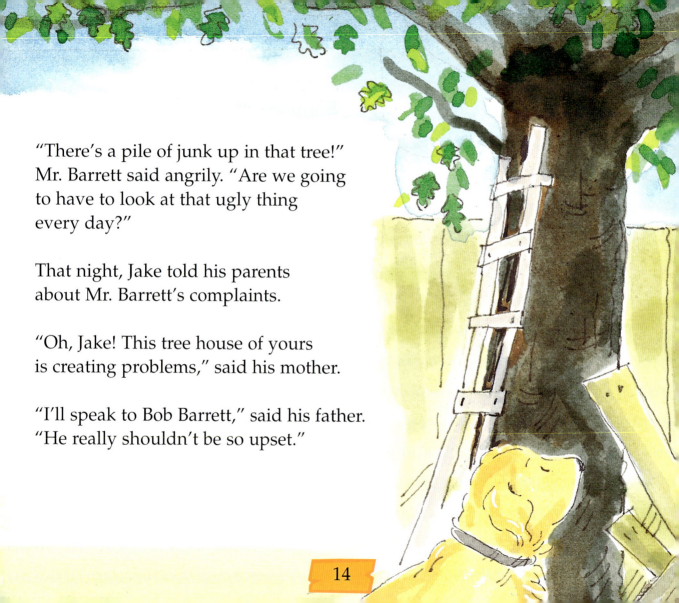

"There's a pile of junk up in that tree!" Mr. Barrett said angrily. "Are we going to have to look at that ugly thing every day?"

That night, Jake told his parents about Mr. Barrett's complaints.

"Oh, Jake! This tree house of yours is creating problems," said his mother.

"I'll speak to Bob Barrett," said his father. "He really shouldn't be so upset."

Jake's father went out the door.
He thought he could make Bob Barrett understand.
But when he came back, he wasn't smiling.

"Bob's not happy. He used to like seeing the sky through the branches. And he still thinks the tree house is a pile of old junk."

Jake's mother looked at Jake. "Maybe he's right. We thought it was junk when it was in our driveway."

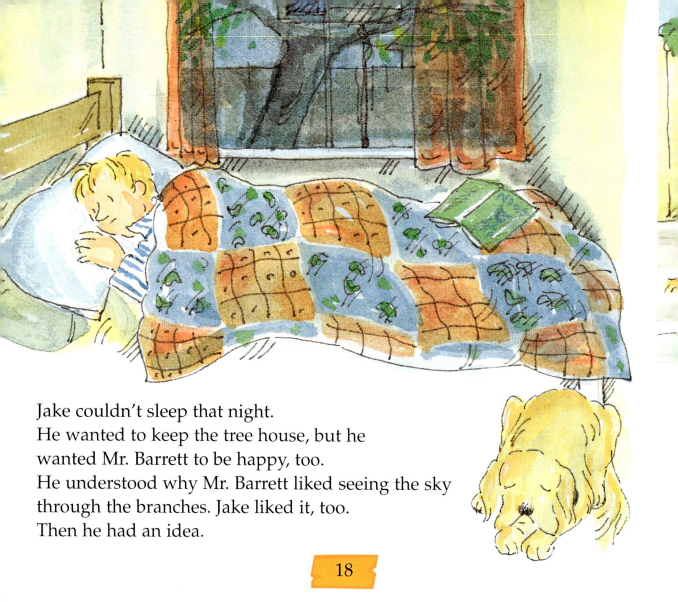

Jake couldn't sleep that night.
He wanted to keep the tree house, but he wanted Mr. Barrett to be happy, too.
He understood why Mr. Barrett liked seeing the sky through the branches. Jake liked it, too.
Then he had an idea.

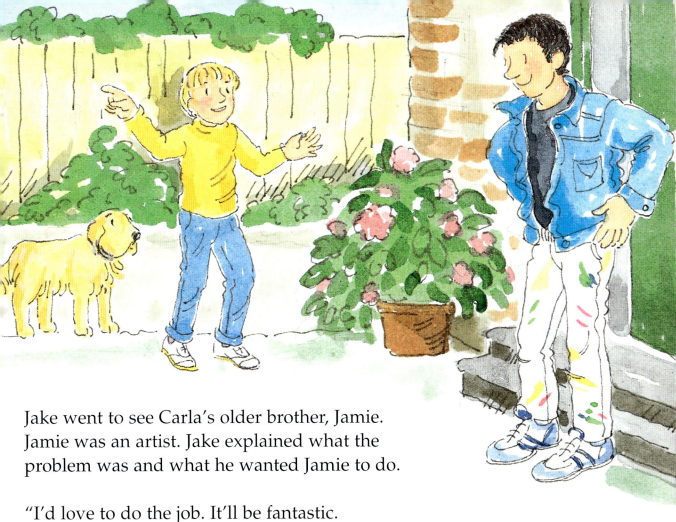

Jake went to see Carla's older brother, Jamie. Jamie was an artist. Jake explained what the problem was and what he wanted Jamie to do.

"I'd love to do the job. It'll be fantastic. Don't worry about it, Jake."

All the next day, Jake was out with his parents. He worried about his plan and hoped that it was working.

The result was better than Jake had expected. Jamie had completely transformed the tree house.

Jake's parents looked up in amazement. "Well, I wonder what Bob Barrett will say about that," Jake's father said with a smile.

Several days later, Mr. Barrett came with two presents for Jake.

"They're for the tree house," he explained.

One was a striped hammock, and the second was a sign that Mr. Barrett had made. It read, *In the Clouds*. Jake thought that was great.

Later, as Jake was lying on his hammock, he listened to the wind in the leaves. Through the branches, he could see the sky.

At last Jake could relax and enjoy his special place in the clouds.